Ten Family B
in Devon

Chips Barber

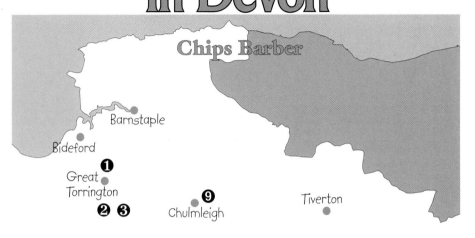

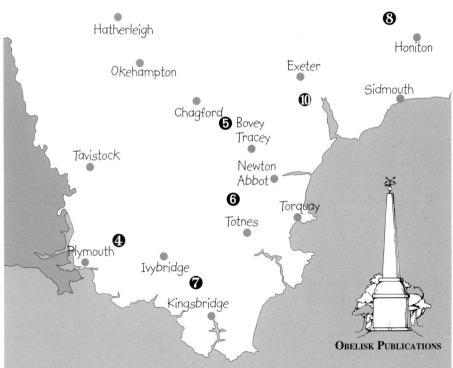

Barnstaple

Bideford

❶
Great
Torrington

❷ ❸

Chulmleigh ❾

Tiverton

Hatherleigh

❽

Honiton

Okehampton

Exeter

Sidmouth

❿

Chagford

❺ Bovey
Tracey

Tavistock

Newton
Abbot

❻

Torquay

Totnes

Plymouth ❹

Ivybridge

❼

Kingsbridge

OBELISK PUBLICATIONS

ALSO BY THE AUTHOR:

Ten Family Walks on Dartmoor
Ten Family Walks in East Devon • Six Short Pub Walks on Dartmoor
Short Circular Walks in and around Sidmouth • Walks on and around Woodbury Common
Diary of a Dartmoor Walker • Diary of a Devonshire Walker
The Great Little Dartmoor Book • The Great Little Exeter Book
The Great Little Totnes Book • The Great Little Plymouth Book • The Great Little Chagford Book
Made in Devon • The Dartmoor Quiz Book • Place-Names in Devon • An A to Z of Devon Dialect
Dark & Dastardly Dartmoor • The Ghosts of Exeter • Haunted Pubs in Devon
Weird & Wonderful Dartmoor • Ghastly & Ghostly Devon
Sidmouth in Colour • Exmouth in Colour • Plymouth in Colour • Dawlish and Dawlish Warren in Colour
Beautiful Exeter • Colourful Dartmoor • Colourful Cockington • Topsham in Colour
The South Hams in Colour • Torbay in Colour – Torquay, Paignton, Brixham
Sidmouth Past and Present • Topsham Past and Present • Honiton Past and Present
Around & About Sidmouth • Around & About Seaton and Beer
Around & About Salcombe • Around & About Teignmouth
Around & About Hope Cove and Thurlestone • Around & About Burgh Island and Bigbury Bay
Around & About Tavistock • Around & About Roborough Down • Around & About Lustleigh
Around & About The Haldon Hills – Revisited • The Lost City of Exeter – Revisited
Dawlish and Dawlish Warren • The South Hams • Torquay • Paignton • Brixham
From The Dart to The Start • Dartmouth and Kingswear • Cranmere Pool – The First Dartmoor Letterbox
Brixham of Yesteryear, Parts I, II and III • Pinhoe of Yesteryear, Parts I and II
Princetown of Yesteryear, Parts I and II • The Teign Valley of Yesteryear, Parts I and II
Widecombe – A Visitor's Guide • Bickleigh – A Visitor's Guide
Newton Ferrers and Noss Mayo • Along The Otter • Along The Tavy • Along The Avon
Railways on and around Dartmoor • Devon's Railways of Yesteryear
Chagford of Yesteryear • Dartmoor of Yesteryear • Exminster of Yesteryear • Dartmouth of Yesteryear
Heavitree of Yesteryear • Sidmouth of Yesteryear • Whipton of Yesteryear
Plymouth Hoe • Tiverton • From Brixham…with love • The Story of Hallsands
The Story of Dawlish Warren • Dawlish of Yesteryear • Discovering Devon…Dawlish
Walk the East Devon Coast – Lyme Regis to Lympstone
Walk the South Devon Coast – Dawlish Warren to Dartmouth
Walk the South Hams Coast – Dartmouth to Salcombe
Walk the South Hams Coast – Salcombe to Plymouth

OTHER TITLES FROM OBELISK PUBLICATIONS INCLUDE:

A Secret Circle, *Deryck Seymour*
The Templer Way, *Derek Beavis* • Walks in the Totnes Countryside, *Bob Mann*
Walks in The South Hams • Pub Walks in and around The Haldon Hills, *Brian Carter*
Nine Short Pub Walks in and around Torbay, *Brian Carter*
Walks in the Shadow of Dartmoor • Walks in Tamar and Tavy Country, *Denis McCallum*
Walks in the Chagford Countryside • The A to Z of Dartmoor Tors, *Terry Bound*
Circular Walks on Eastern Dartmoor, *Liz Jones* • The Dartmoor Mountain Bike Guide, *Peter Barnes*
Dartmoor Letterboxing–A Beginner's Guide, *Kevin Weall*

We have over 180 Devon titles. For a current list, please send SAE to
Obelisk Publications at the address below. Tel: (01392) 468556

PLATE ACKNOWLEDGEMENTS

All sketch maps drawn from an out-of-copyright source by Sally Barber
Thanks to Dennis Bater for pages 9 and 10 (top)
All other photographs by or belonging to Chips Barber

First published in 2004 by
Obelisk Publications, 2 Church Hill, Pinhoe, Exeter, Devon EX4 9ER
Designed and typeset by Sally Barber
Printed in Great Britain
by Avocet Press, Cullompton, Devon

INTRODUCTION

Let us start with an important point. Even though this book is entitled 'family bike rides', you are not obliged to take any children with you! Mine ("Sorry, too busy!") couldn't be persuaded. For the purpose of this book, the definition of a 'family bike ride' is one tailored to the needs of the occasional cyclist who enjoys a pleasurable, non-marathon outing in the country, generally avoiding busy roads and long, steep, demoralising hills. However, such is the nature of the county's hilly topography, it is inevitable that some of the circular rides in this book will require more 'pedal-power' than others.

A deliberate attempt has been made to spread the routes around the county, but Devon is big place; it's a long way from east to west and even further from north to south. The distribution of routes is also governed by the fact that there are areas less suited to 'family' cycling. Several of the rides are along former railway lines, a number are on quiet country lanes, whilst one is beside a river and canal… so, if you are passing, don't drop in!

As a very rough guide, most of these outings are intended to last between two and four hours. I travelled at a sedate (one could even say sedated) speed and was in no rush, so the rides are in no way up to 'Tour de France' demands. To make them more interesting, many snippets of local history are included.

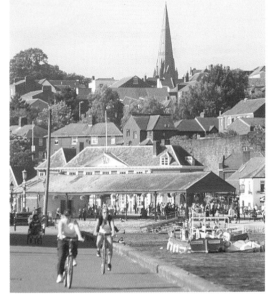

Where necessary, some basic sketch maps are included for those rides where the route descriptions are more complicated, and where it's easier to go astray. There are parts of Devon where the signposts were removed during the Second World War and still haven't been replaced! In the case of the other rides, maps shouldn't be necessary, other than for locating the start. However, I would still strongly recommend a small investment in a decent road map of the county to give you a better idea of what each outing entails. Reading the description before you set off will enable you to be reasonably well briefed. It will also help if you are planning a full day out in that particular part of the county.

Although the routes have been chosen carefully for your enjoyment, it is essential that you take great care and cycle in single file, particularly on those rides which are along public highways.

Please make sure that you can be clearly seen by other road users. This is one of the few activities where it is trendy to be ultra-conspicuous and it accords that 'loud' is safer! Camouflaged cyclists are always more likely to 'cop it' than those who don suitable fluorescent gear.

You should always protect your extremely soft head with a hard helmet. On these ten outings, I was lucky enough not to need the bicycle tools, crash helmet, puncture repair kit, spare inner tube or basic first-aid kit, all of which I usually took with me, but *you* may not be quite as fortunate. Make sure that your bicycle is in good order, particularly the brakes and tyres.

Wherever possible I have tried to suggest vehicle parking places where there are no charges. Always beware of car thieves, who, if they don't steal your vehicle, may attempt to relieve you of your valuables. Conceal these or take them with you.

On that cautionary note, it's time to hit the saddle with a fairly gentle introductory ride.

❶ Great Torrington to Instow and back – Tarka Country

There are several bike-hire centres in North Devon; as I didn't have my own bike at the outset of this book, I chose to hire one from the shop at the former railway station at Torrington. As a customer I could park here, but anyone following this ride using their own bike is advised to use the large free car park on Torrington Common. This is located on the A386 high above the Torridge valley, at the top of Station Hill, opposite the junction with Limer's Hill and about half a mile to the west of the town centre. If you have the relevant OS map, the grid reference is SS486194.

It is said that from this high spot more church towers can be seen than from any other vantage point in Devon. On a more practical level, there are toilets here, the last for quite a few miles.

Great care should be exercised in descending the steep hill by the narrow pavement on the far, or left, side of the busy road from Great Torrington to Bideford. The descent is necessary in order to reach the former Torrington railway station building, which has been turned into the aptly named Puffing Billy pub.

The former railway line from Torrington to Bideford (and beyond) is the cycle route to be followed. This is now an off-road ride away from traffic, through terrific valley and estuary countryside. There is the bonus that it's impossible to get lost...

In the first two miles the River Torridge is crossed three times. The first two bridges are soon passed, the cycle route being more direct along the Torridge valley than the meandering river. The second is close to a lovely weir, where it's not uncommon to see rock climbers on the hillside a little way downstream. If you are lucky with the time of year, you may see salmon leaping this obstruction.

At the third bridge, pause and glance left upstream to a tall, elegant five-arched aqueduct. This was built to carry the six-mile long James Green-engineered Rolle Canal, or at least part of it. It was opened in 1823; from 1827 to its close in 1871 its principal function was the transportation of clays from the Petrockstow basin, an area to the south of here to be explored on the next two rides. When the foundation stone of the aqueduct was laid, a cannon was fired from a nearby hillside and the boom reverberated around the steep valley sides like a roll of thunder.

Continuing on the level way, to the left the main road to Bideford runs close by but presents no real intrusion, whilst to the right is the sprawling village of Weare Giffard. Some of the houses have had to be raised up, as the Torridge is prone to flooding.

Above a sharp bend in the river there is a good view of the church and the adjacent (haunted) Weare Giffard Hall. Sir Walter Giffard passed away in 1243 but, according to some, even now he

Weare Gifford

slowly makes his way the short distance from his ancient home to the church. Here his ghostly apparition bangs on the enormously heavy door. As if by magic, this opens and the knight enters, only to fade away… until the next time.

The Torridge at Bideford

There used to be shipyards near Weare Giffard. The hulls of the vessels were built here, then floated downstream through the widest arch of Bideford Bridge – which we shall see in a few miles – to be fitted out and finished in deeper water.

Children seem to love going through the next feature – a long, lit tunnel with a concrete floor.

We have been riding through 'Tarka Country' whilst following the old railway. *Tarka the Otter* was first published in 1927. Next we pass Landcross, where the author Henry Williamson got married (for the first time) in May 1925. It is one of those bizarre coincidences that on the same day that the film-makers shot Tarka's death scene – 13 August 1977 – Henry Williamson passed away.

At Landcross Viaduct the river assumes the full appearance of a tidal estuary. For the rest of the ride to Bideford and beyond we follow the east bank. About 500 yards further on, by the right-hand side of the cycle way, is a memorial to the RAF crew who lost their lives in a plane crash on 7 March 1945.

Bideford Station, now a railway museum, is next; please take care when riding along the platform. There's no need to hurry; this is the one train you can't miss! I stopped here to photograph these beautifully and artistically sculptured passengers. A work of art by Bideford's talented John Butler, they were created in 1995 from railway sleepers, and went under the title of *Waiting for the Train*. It is sad to relate that a few weeks after my visit some mindless morons vandalised them.

A hump-backed bridge leads you safely past the back of Bideford's famous Royal Hotel. Built in 1688, this was where Charles Kingsley wrote parts of his famous book *Westward Ho!*, which was published in 1855.

The railway line between Bideford and Barnstaple was opened on 29 October that same year. A staggering 4,000 passengers travelled on the 'Bideford Extension Railway' on its first day. The running of the line was taken over by the London and South Western Railway in 1862 and witnessed further changes. The last passenger train, from Barnstaple to Torrington, ran in October 1965, thereby ending a history of 110 years of railway service. This loss is now our gain.

Instow

We are now joined by the South West Coast Path, sharing our route. Many intrepid walkers like to plod this way, so exercise care when coming up behind them; a friendly ring on the bell warns them of your presence. It's also mildly amusing to see them jump, but as Devon President of the Ramblers' Association, I really shouldn't say that! From a walker's perspective, it's nice to know that cyclists have seen you and are taking care not to run you down.

Bideford is soon left behind and the towering, cantilever Torridge Bridge dominates the view. The cycle way passes beneath it and on along the side of the estuary. The famous shipbuilding village of Appledore will be spied on the opposite shore.

Our route passes through a cutting and beside a boatyard before reaching Instow. The signal box was the first building of its type in the United Kingdom to be listed as of architectural and historical merit.

Instow was about as far as I wanted – or was prepared – to go on a trial outing. It is some $8^{1}/_{2}$ miles from Torrington, so around 17 miles would be covered before the return journey was completed. I deemed this to be enough for a first day's cycling in over 30 years!

Bideford Station

With careful planning, a picnic on the sandy beach at Instow or a visit to a pub or café could be enjoyed. The seafront is nearby.

On the way up little attention was paid to Bideford, but it is a town steeped in history, so certainly merits a short detour on the return ride. Simply come off this cycle way at Bideford's former station and cross the ancient Long Bridge.

The way back to Torrington is the same way that we came but the views will be different. You may recognise some of the cyclists you pass, as you might have seen them go by in the opposite direction earlier in the day.

All that remains to be done on reaching the former Torrington Station is to leave the line and further improve your circulation by climbing the steep hill back to the starting point.

❷ Petrockstow to Torrington and back – Clay Country

For this ride of about 14 miles, the starting point is Petrockstow's former railway station (SS517107). There is a small free car park, and the remains of a platform here. The car park is located by following the A386 between Hatherleigh and Torrington. Travelling northwards, turn left a few miles beyond Meeth; travelling southwards, turn right just after passing through Merton. The 'station' is about three-quarters of a mile down this road on the left-hand side, by a junction with another minor road.

Like the last ride, it is along an extension of the same former railway line, but unlike it has some steeper gradients. This route takes us back to Torrington, but from the opposite direction and through completely different countryside.

As a yardstick, if the ride is good enough for a Mayor of Hatherleigh, then it's good enough for me! Dennis Bater has held this honour several times; when we talked of potential rides in his home territory, he recommended this one with immense enthusiasm. So keen was he that not only did he lend me his spare bike, he also insisted on joining me.

From the car park, carefully cross the road to pass onto the former railway line beyond. The initiation is gentle, but after rain there can be wet spots where surface water accumulates. This is not at all surprising because this natural basin has been the source for ball clay for some considerable time; as most gardeners know, clay soils don't drain very well. Ball clay is so called because it was originally extracted by workers using spikes – the clay drawn from the ground had a ball-like appearance.

The green embankments appearing a little further on mark the edge of the Marland quarries. Beyond them is the village of Merton, its church a recognisable landmark. It was here that the founder of Merton College, Oxford, Walter de Merton, was born. We, too, can advance by 'degrees' along this well-defined track through gentle, green and pleasant countryside.

The ruins of a former small railway hut are passed on the left; the fireplace is just about visible. Dennis Bater reckoned that this was where railwaymen kept maintenance tools and had their snacks; these sometimes lasted so long that they merged into one another to form a grand binge!

Away from traffic, there is a lot of wildlife to be seen. We saw a fox, several varieties of butterflies, and many species of bird – much as one would expect on the 'Tarka Trail'.

The line runs by a small belt of woodland and over a small watercourse. After a while the entrance to the Marland clay works is passed, the buildings giving an industrial presence to what, so far, has been a rural scene. Beyond, the track drops a little to pass along one of the wetter sections of the route, with water-filled ditches either side.

Soon the track crosses the River Mere (hence Merton), a tributary of the mighty Torridge. Just beyond is another road. To the right lies Great Potheridge, which is part of the Clinton estates. A family called Monk owned Great Potheridge from the time of Henry II and one of their number achieved great things. Born 6 December 1608, George Monk (or Monck; d. 1670) was a soldier through and through, tough and uncompromising but so fair in his dealings that he fully deserved the cognomen 'Honest George Monk'. He was held in the highest esteem and was bestowed with many official titles: Duke of Albemarle, Earl of Torrington and Baron Monk of Potheridge. In 1666, when the Great Fire of London was raging, it was said that had George not been at sea engaging the Dutch in combat, then the city would not have been so badly burned.

A short way further on is the former Dunsbear Halt, which is rather overgrown. A steady climb to Yarde follows. This is a former mining and quarrying hamlet at the top of a long but pleasant incline.

Yarde Villa is a yellow-brick 'Addams Family'-style building with a neat weather-vane bearing two owls; one is bigger than the other, but neither gives a hoot. Here, too, are the remains of Yarde Halt. The days have long since gone when clay workers waited to catch the train to travel to work on the original 'Torrington & Marland' light railway, which opened in 1880. It didn't provide the safest of journeys: there were fatalities. The line was later redeveloped to a standard gauge and extended to become the North Devon & Cornwall Junction Light Railway, which was abbreviated to NDCJLR. Opened in the summer of 1925, this line ran $20^{1}/_{2}$ miles between Torrington and Halwill Junction; the latter was in the middle of nowhere, but was where several lines converged.

Just up the slope above Yarde, at the top of a damp cutting, is a point called 'Summit'. This was the highest point on the line, hence its name.

From here to Torrington it's almost all downhill, but the temptation to whizz along is tempered by signs telling you to go slowly as a lot of ramblers – and dog walkers – also use this thoroughfare. The rhythm of cycling is also broken by a number of gates that stand in the way. Goodness knows how tandems cope in negotiating their way through them!

The next minor road is passed over, rather than across, as the track drops through attractive woodlands and above a small stream.

A redeveloped former mill called Watergate is eventually reached, but there were no 'President's Men' around when we passed by. There are picnic tables beside the line should you wish to sample the delights of an alfresco meal. Birds and beasties will devour leftovers, but remember to take home any rubbish.

The track goes ever-onward, across yet another road and past the remains of another short platform, to enter what is probably the prettiest part of this ride. The thickly wooded valley of Pencleave is deep and sheltered. ('Cleave' is a steep-sided valley, as at Lustleigh Cleave, Belstone Cleave and Tavy Cleave, all on Dartmoor.)

The vista opens up as the Torridge valley is joined. Torrington's great hill or common stands sentinel ahead.

The viaduct over the River Torridge is an impressive structure. It is a breathtaking way to reach the base of the hill on which this historic North Devon town stands.

We settled for a breather and an ice cream at the former station (Puffing Billy), but you may want to burn up excess energy by climbing the hill again to visit the nearby town.

Perhaps a visit to 'Torrington 1646', a Civil War 'cavalier experience', or some of the other attractions would help make it a more complete day out.

Refreshed, educated or even entertained, retrace your way to Petrockstow. The journey back involves quite a long and steepish haul from Watergate to Summit, but once that is passed, it's all plain cycling back to the start at Petrockstow. The village pub is the Laurels Inn; it lies about a mile away from the platform. Just the ticket!

If you are curious – nay, mystified – to note that I have failed to mention the numerous wonderful works of art along the way, it is because my cycle ride pre-dated their arrival.

Have a look at your map to check the spelling of Petrockstow. I looked at several in my possession and also surfed the internet. About half the references have it ending with an 'e'. Even the road signs in this lovely little village are divided on this matter.

8

❸ Return to the Petrockstow Basin – More of the Same!

It is seven years since I first cycled this route; since then it has been extended from Petrockstow to Meeth. There is even talk of taking the cycle trail all the way on to Bude. That would be marvellous. The starting point is the same as for the last ride.

I met up with Dennis Bater again. By now I had my own bike, a modest machine with a very well-cushioned seat. It was the sort that, when I dismounted after a lengthy ride, *didn't* feel as if it were still in place! Ah, bliss.

For those looking for an easy and pleasant route, this will take about an hour. There is potential for making it longer if need be. Should this be the case, then the latter part of the ride will be, for the most part, along relatively quiet country lanes. This part of Devon being less populous, the high-hedged lanes are generally free of any significant volume of traffic.

Instead of heading north-westwards, as in the second ride, simply set off in the opposite direction, along the platform of the former Petrockstow station and down onto the track bed of the former railway.

Away to the right, on the hillside, there are glimpses of Petrockstow (or Stow St Petrock, as it was sometimes styled in Victorian times). Its lovely church of St Petrock makes a distinct landmark. Although a Celtic saint normally more closely associated with Brittany, Wales and Cornwall, there are many churches dedicated to Petrock in Devon. His name is the Celtic equivalent of Peter. Born in Wales, he was converted by St Patrick, a fellow Celt.

Petrock was an aristocratic bishop. It is understood that he travelled to various parts of Devon with his disciples and relations, founding cells of worship staffed by monks. Some of these later evolved into parish churches: Petrockstow, Lydford, Dartmouth, Farringdon, and Harford on southern Dartmoor. His most spectacular self-discipline was to immerse himself often in cold water for lengthy periods!

After about half a mile, the track crosses over a significant stream. Just beyond, it reaches a junction marked by an unusual iron mile-post, one of a thousand sponsored by the Royal Bank of Scotland; if you have followed the national cycle network, you will be familiar with these signs.

Here, turn sharp right to leave the railway. We are 2¼ miles from Meeth and 8¾ miles from Great Torrington.

The next section is lovely. Still surfaced specifically for our purposes, the track runs beside the Little Mere river, its bed cut in clay. The clay presence becomes more obvious when, having crossed a stream, the track we are on is bisected by a broad road linking clay quarries on both sides. A sign warns to beware of 'Heavy Plant Crossing'; you could look out for an enormous cyclist-gobbling aspidistra, but it is more likely to be an ugly piece of industrial machinery!

To the right, beyond an area of green belt, is a broad quarry track. This will soon be left behind after another of those 'thousand' signs is encountered. Meeth is just 1 mile away. Continue through a gate to discover two fords.

Beyond is a steep slope, which leads back up to the former railway. However, it isn't rejoined; the path runs beside it to Meeth Halt. Should you wish to use the waiting room, you may do so; it's an ideal place to enjoy your refreshments.

If you are keen for a more serious drink or a substantial meal, there is a pub in this tiny village; it is to the left, a short way along the main road. This is the 14th-century Bull and Dragon. If you choose to make a visit, take great care and beware of speeding drivers.

If you now want to take the soft and safer option, the easier way to return to the start is to turn around and retrace the route. However, if you wish to make this a more circular ride, and you don't mind some steep hills, then from Meeth Halt turn right onto the main road. Although not the busiest highway, extreme care should be taken. Proceed in single file, and hog the far left side of the road. Stay with it for about a mile, until a road leads off straight ahead at a point where the main road

swings sharply left. This is Friar's Hele Cross. The lane ahead will take you around the edge of this clay basin. Ultimately, 2 miles further on, having travelled straight on at Ash Cross, it will bring you into Petrockstow village. The occasional view over the Petrockstow Basin is glorious, particularly in the late afternoon when the sun backlights this scene.

Having negotiated some ups and downs to reach the village, the church may be visited. Plus, of course, there is below it the aforementioned pub – the Laurels, a 17th-century coaching house on the original route from Launceston to Lynton. Once known as the White Hart, it has had many other uses: magistrates' court, home for fallen women, lodging house, coffee tavern and private dwelling. It reopened as a welcoming public house in the mid-1970s.

The ride is almost done. If, however, you still feel the need to ride some more, an outing along the undulating country lanes to the west of Petrockstow may be considered. The ride to Shebbear, where you can see the famed 'Devil's Stone', is just under five miles each way; with some great views across to Dartmoor, it will probably satisfy that need. It is a lane ride through Devon countryside at its peaceful best.

To complete the scheduled route, about a quarter of a mile beyond the church of St Petrock turn right at a crossroads and descend the hill. In about half a mile of easy riding you will get back to Petrockstow's former halt. Should you choose the easy option, the distance is about 6 miles, but if you come back along roads it is about 8. If you add an extension to Shebbear and back, it is 18 miles.

❹ From Plymouth to Dartmoor and back!

Having explored some of North Devon's cycling delights, it's time to consider what the south of the county has to offer. The starting point is yet another free car park (SX505545), but one with no facilities. In order to get to it from the Plymouth city direction, cross Laira Bridge on the A379, over the Plym, and at the end of it turn left. If you approach along the A379 from the Yealmpton direction, turn right at the traffic lights just before this long bridge. Whichever way you come, it is a humpy-bumpy, untidy road that you turn onto. However, this will soon be forgotten when you are nestled on those perfectly fitting saddles and bound for the quieter, distant hills of Dartmoor.

There is one practical consideration to ponder before setting off. A visit to the pub at the farthest end of the route, although recommended, is not obligatory and, in good weather, a picnic on Roborough Down is a pleasant alternative. But, as there are no shops along the immediate way (unless a detour is made), you will need to stock up on goodies before beginning the ride.

The 'business end' of the River Plym is below Laira Bridge, where the waters are deeper. It is said that the estuary became silted many centuries ago after tin miners on Dartmoor disturbed the ground. The materials were carried in suspension by the fast-moving Plym, but on reaching the lowland sank to the bottom of the river. The stretch of estuary that we will soon skirt is therefore relatively shallow. Where we park it will appear like mud flats if it is low water, but more like a lake if the tide is high. Whatever it is when you start, it will be in a different state by the time you return!

Dutch Maids

The first part of this 16-mile ride is along part of the West Devon Way, the first straight being aptly known as 'The Ride'. To the right is Chelson Meadow, drained in 1806 to become a racecourse but, as you will see, something very different today.

After about half a mile, The Ride comes to an abrupt end. At Point Cottage, just beyond a gate, things start to perk up as the grounds of Saltram House (National Trust) are entered. Although we don't see the house, I can tell you that it enjoyed film fame when it featured in the screen adaptation of Jane Austen's *Sense and Sensibility*. However, the lion's share of filming was done on the privately owned Erme estuary.

The track rises and falls as it follows the edge of the Plym. On the right is an amphitheatre, or folly, complete with three faces, one looking decidedly more cheerful than the other two. Ahead is the distinct 'Dutch Maids' roof of Sainsbury's supermarket at Marsh Mills. Although this looks far off, it won't be long before we pass right beside it, albeit on the opposite side of the river.

Soon the river is left behind. Drop down to a gate and a small depression in parkland surroundings. Pass through it, staying with the track until, in a short distance up a slope, a T-junction is met. Turn left here to cycle along to yet another gate, which must be passed through. Here the track drops down and around towards the mighty viaducts that carry the A38 over the Marsh Mills roundabout.

Observant types will have noticed that the Plym estuary has suddenly narrowed. A strategically placed sign points to the Plym Valley, the way for us to go. The cycle way rises to pass over the railway and under the road bridges. The track

skirts the edge of a sports field to reach the main road from Plymouth to Plympton, a conveyor belt of almost non-stop traffic. The good news is that we don't have to take our lives in our hands

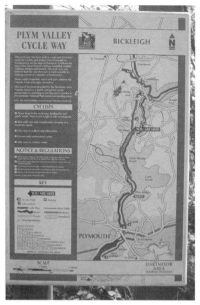

to cross it. Turn right and descend a slope. At the bottom to the right is the Tavistock Junction freight yard, but to the left is a safe passage for us beneath the main road.

Another road is met in a short distance; we need to dismount and cross straight over.

If you are at a loss as to which way to go, just look for an elevated sign!

Pass the Coypool Park & Ride car park to find a narrow track. To the right is the Plym Valley Railway, whose association has, so far, 712 yards of line and many dedicated members. Even though the railway runs out of steam, we don't.

It's good to get back to more rural surroundings, with the Plym on the left, and a disused watercourse on the right. This water-filled ditch was the Cann Quarry Canal, a venture sponsored by the Earl of Morley, who owned the land. The intended engineer was John Smeaton; he designed and built the third Eddystone Lighthouse, which now stands on Plymouth Hoe.

In 1778 Smeaton aired his misgivings about the proposed canal and suggested that a railroad was a better option. Half a century of inactivity followed. In November 1829, a short tub-boat canal opened between Cann Quarry and Marsh Mills; horse-drawn barges were used to carry slates and paving stones along it. Later a tramway was built on the banks beside it and wagons full of the same materials were horse-drawn along the railroad. By then the canal was little more than a leat used to power a flour mill; it 'ground' to a halt in 1920.   *Plym Bridge*

Accessible by passing under the former railway bridge, the ancient stone structure of Plym Bridge merits a visit. The way up onto the former GWR branch to Tavistock is on the car park side of the raised embankment. The steepish access path marks the beginning of several miles of lovely, northwards cycling. As it is heading for the hills, this former branch line gently rises for most of the way.

Cann Viaduct is soon reached, the first of four such structures to be encountered. For several months of the year, the wooded scene around it is predominantly green. Over your right shoulder is the exposed and massive cliff face of Cann Quarry.

Pedalling just a little harder now, head onwards to Riverford Viaduct, built in 1893. This bridge spans a stream that rises a little to the north of Glenholt, close to Plymouth Airport.

Continuing on, Bickleigh Viaduct is easily reached. From here two churches can be seen: the one to your left is Bickleigh; the one ahead, to the right, is Shaugh Prior. Both are featured in another of my books, *Around & About Roborough Down*.

The route instruction is predictable – just keep that gentle therapeutic pedalling motion going as the track continues to gently rise. But what is this? We are soon directed off the railway line and up to a road. A sign tells us that if we want to regain the former railway line, which we do, we shall have to turn left to climb a steep hill. Fortunately it's only a short, sharp rise.

Soon, to the right, a signpost pointing to Shaugh Prior shows us the way to go. We now redress the balance by dropping back down. Around a right-hand bend we meet and greet the railway again and turn left to pick it up. After a few twists the fourth viaduct is reached – Ham Green. Away to the right is the craggy hill known as the Dewerstone.

The edge of Roborough Down

The gradual incline continues towards a substantial former railway platform. In the days before common car ownership, Bank Holiday trains carried thousands of Plymothians to Shaugh Bridge Platform, opened in 1907. Many would alight here, before walking down to Shaugh Bridge to explore the spectacular scenery of this district.

Staying on the railway, an electrically lit 308-yard-long tunnel has to be passed through.

Now in the valley of the Meavy, a tributary of the Plym, we pass the 'weak' Goodameavy Bridge to the right. The line becomes more bumpy and several silver birches have established themselves in the track-bed, so it is 'dodge the tree' time. In a while a sign states that we must leave the railway again. Dismount, pass through a gate on the left, then using a zig-zag path, ascend the steep scarp slope of Roborough Down.

The path leads up and over the down; red arrows (of the non-flying variety) reveal the way to go. On meeting a rough track, turn left. A road is reached within a short distance. Just a little way up it is our destination – the Skylark Inn at Clearbrook – and time for a well-earned rest.

Refreshed, it's time to return to the start. There shouldn't be a problem retracing the way. You may like to make more of an excursion out of it and visit Shaugh Bridge. You may even want to go for a game of tenpin bowling at Plympton, or take time out to look round Saltram House.

If you found the going slightly tough on the way up to Dartmoor, then take heart that it is mostly downhill on the way back: therefore a quicker journey. Having got some momentum going, and that doesn't happen too often, it took me about half the time to make the return journey.

Saltram House

❺ Dartmoor – Up Downs and Round Reservoirs

This is a Dartmoor ride of about 12 miles, encompassing some spectacular scenery. The starting point is on Mardon Down, an upland area of isolated moorland just over a mile to the north-east of Moretonhampstead.

There is a gravel-surfaced, free car park at SX763873 which can accommodate about 20 to 30 cars. It is rarely full. To get to it, take the Moretonhampstead–Steps Bridge road. A quarter of a mile south of Doccombe, at Cossick Cross, head northwards to reach a cattle grid. At the junction just yards past it, turn left. Follow the road around the hillside, which overlooks Moretonhampstead, to reach the car-park; it lies about half a mile further on, on the right-hand side of the road.

With open moorlands, forests and reservoirs along the way, the route is along narrow but just-about surfaced lanes.

It was a beautiful summer's day in November when I did this ride. Although late in the year, the sun shone from a cloudless deep blue sky; there wasn't a breath of wind and it was warm enough to cycle without any extra cumbersome clothing. Although the rest of Dartmoor was relatively busy that day, with folks enjoying the unseasonably good weather, on this excursion I saw only four moving cars and a tractor in the 12 miles cycled.

This is one of those elongated 'circular' rides where there are far more right turns than left, particularly in the first few hundred yards, where there are several.

From the car park turn right; just yards down the slope, at the first junction, turn right again towards Clifford Bridge. In next to no time, take the road that forks off to the right to climb the edge of the open down.

After a gentle upwards incline of several hundred yards, a triangular green is met. On it is a single signpost. This tells us from whence we came but not where we are bound. Turn right and continue to go up the down (if you know what I mean).

Having reached more of a level, vegetation masks the view of the valley to the left. However, the occasional gap yields a glimpse of the top of the combe that leads down to the picturesque hamlet of Doccombe. For a hill settlement, it is one of the most sheltered places in Devon.

Soon we reach a junction, with a cattle grid to the left. Cross it in the time-honoured juddery fashion, then proceed along the road. Ignore a road leading off to the right; stay with this thoroughfare to Cossick Cross.

Here several lanes converge. Beyond the junction, take the left of the two roads. The signpost points to Blackingstone Rock. Several hundred yards along this lane, at a house called Didworthy, where granite posts mark an entrance between two roads, bear left and use your improving pedal power to ascend a short, steep rise. Just over the brow of the hill, past the entrance to Blackenstone Quarry (original spelling), is another multi-route junction. It had a damaged signpost when I passed by. If it's still there, turn right here for 'Chr' and 'H'. Locals will know that this refers to Christow and Hennock, so won't need the signpost. Strangers to the district probably won't, so will have to work out what they represent. 'The Dartmoor Way' follows a similar route to the one we are following for the next miles, this being signed by newer, neater, modern brown and white signs.

Almost immediately on the left is a point of pedestrian access to the isolated mass of Blackingstone Rock. Should you choose to climb this large outcrop, there is an iron ladder to facilitate an easy passage to the summit. It is well worth the short detour: the 360-degree view is superb. Legend has it that King Arthur once did this and exchanged projectiles with the Devil, who had elected to scale the aptly named Heltor Rock, a few miles distant.

Kennick Reservoir

The lane wends its way around a bend to reach a most attractive avenue of trees. Ignoring a small road leading off to the left, well beyond it, enjoy the next mile as it is the easiest one on the ride. We are on an upland tableland, a plateau broken only by the small streams that feed the triple reservoirs of Tottiford, Trenchford and Kennick. Indeed it is the last one that we shall meet first, but only after we have passed Kennick Barn and continued straight ahead at the following T-junction.

From there it is downhill to Kennick, in my opinion the most picturesque of the three upland man-made lakes in this 'neck of the woods'.

The road skirts the reservoir, then crosses the causeway that ponds back its waters. To the right you will spy the upper reaches of Tottiford reservoir, viewed with tunnel vision down a long narrow corridor through the trees.

It is now a case of uphill for a while as the road passes between woods to climb away from the water. The next junction is met in about half a mile. The way to go is hard right. The signpost points to 'Bovey': Bovey Tracey, not North Bovey!

The next half a mile is also very easy cycling as it is mostly downhill or along the flat. In recent years a great swathe of trees has been felled, which allows a view over to the twin peaks of distant Haytor, Dartmoor's most visited tor. Ignore a road that runs down from the left and continue ahead up the rise. Within yards is another junction where our way turns right. However, if by now you crave civilisation and hanker after liquid refreshment, then you can continue straight on for Hennock, where the Palk Arms awaits your custom. Any extension of this nature adds some healthy ups and downs and an extra

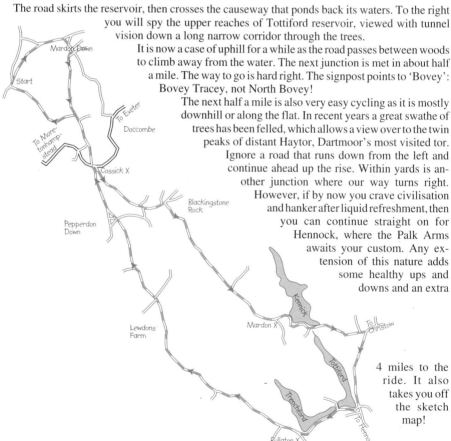

4 miles to the ride. It also takes you off the sketch map!

Trenchford Reservoir

Having turned right, this is the darkest part of the ride, as the forest canopy creates a twilight world. It is only a short stretch and things lighten up where Tottiford and Trenchford reservoirs meet. On reaching the causeway between the two, turn left to follow the road that skirts the southern edge of Trenchford Reservoir.

Pass over another dam: water to the right, chasm to the left. The difference in levels indicates how deep the water is. The road curves right beyond this to ascend the slope to a car park and picnic area at Bullaton Cross. This is an excellent place to take a breather. Although we are past the halfway point in miles covered, going back to the start includes more ups and downs than we have thus far experienced. It is therefore a good time to recharge the batteries, ready for the more demanding challenge that awaits.

Having perhaps rested a while, our way from the car park entrance is uphill to the right. Little route detail is required for the next few miles; it is simply a case of staying with this road all the way back to Cossick Cross, about 3 miles away. There are some long drags up, matched by some downhill stretches. The route passes the entrances to several isolated properties including Lower Elsford, Elsford and Lewdons Farm.

Having pedalled steadily for a few miles from Bullaton Cross, we drop down to a T-junction, four miles from Hennock, where the joint properties of Rose Cottage and Moorlands lie to the left. Beyond this, and still straight ahead, is the steepest and longest climb of the ride. It may be only scant consolation, but towards the top it does dwindle to a gentler gradient.

The reward is an incredible view. From the heights of Pepperdon Down there is a magnificent westwards panorama taking in the range of Dartmoor hills, from Cawsand Hill (Cosdon) in the north to Haytor on the south-eastern margin.

Beyond Pepperdon to Cossick Cross, about half a mile away, is the longest descent of the ride. Cossick Cross should now be familiar territory. Carefully cross the road and head along the lane opposite. Ignore the first turning to the left; ride as far as the cattle grid that we rattled over a few hours earlier. Here, turn left to climb over the south-western shoulder of this part of Mardon Down.

Once the road's high point has been achieved, we go along the level and then sharply downhill back to the starting point. Don't get too carried away and hurtle down this slope – you may just overshoot the car park!

❻ Ipplepen, Denbury and Broadhempston – 'The Secret Circle'

It was always my intention to include a cycle route within reach of the large populace of South Devon, but there is an acute shortage of good 'family rides' in and around the major resorts. Having spent quite a time studying maps, I chose this cycle route in an area that was described in a book by Deryck Seymour as 'The Secret Circle'. The 'secret' stems from the fact that few tourists (or even Devonians) know of these places. The 'circle' is an approximation to the area bordered by the A38 to the north-west; the Buckfast–Totnes road to the south-west; the Totnes–Newton Abbot road to the east; and, to complete the circle, the Newton Abbot–Ashburton road to the north.

Within this defined area is some gorgeous countryside, crisscrossed by a maze of backwater lanes. It is sprinkled with attractive villages: Landscove, Staverton, Littlehempston, Denbury, Broadhempston and Ipplepen. The last three all feature in this ride.

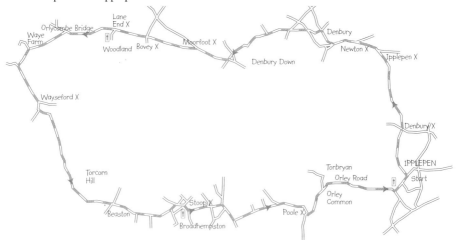

The start and finish is at Ipplepen, which lies just off the main Newton Abbot to Totnes road (A381). Usually it is possible to park in or close to the triangular area around the Ipplepen village war memorial. There are a post office and two pubs nearby: the Plough Inn and the Wellington. But if you want a drink, you really ought to work for it! If you are planning to have a pub meal or bar snack on the way round, there are several possible pubs from which to choose. With flexible opening times, it would be as well to telephone to enquire first.

It would also be sensible to take only seasoned cyclists with you; they will need to be able to cope with fairly steep hills.

A signpost opposite the post office points the way to Denbury, which is the first village to make for. We start with a short downhill freewheel along North Street. At the first fork, bear right up Townsend Hill, but keep a lookout for villagers being taken for a walk by their dogs!

Denbury Cross is soon reached. Ignore the turn left into Moor Road, and proceed almost straight on (the junction is staggered) towards Denbury.

The surface is best described as 'agricultural' in places. The lane undulates to Ipplepen Cross, with one steepish, twisting downward slope on this section.

As this junction is eventually approached, look straight ahead to the far horizons to spy distinct Haytor.

Bear left at Ipplepen Cross. At Newton Cross bear left again. Denbury is about a quarter of a mile away.

Should you seek refreshment so early in the ride, the Union Inn beside the village green provides the first opportunity. If not, follow the chevrons around to the right, then head along South Street and into the centre of the village. Here there is a redundant conduit on the central crossroads. In spring and summer Denbury is a floral delight, with its attractive cottages garlanded in flowers.

Having reached this point, turn left to head out of 'town' along West Street. This leads towards Woodland, which we shall reach later. At the next forking of roads bear left along Woodland Road. Soon you will see Woodland's church tower in the distance ahead.

The large wooded hill to our left is Denbury Down. Denbury means 'the stronghold of the men of Devon' and is an ancient settlement. According to legend, it is here "They buried a King with a golden crown... there's more gold to be found... than is ever found in London Town." Did I forget to tell you to bring your pickaxes and swag bags? Don't bother – it's only a legend. Similar Devonshire legends have ghost ladies protecting buried treasure. There is even a flying dragon doing surveillance security work on two other 'treasure-laden' sites in East Devon, apparently.

Continue along the lane until a crossroads is reached at Brambleoak Cross, about half a mile from Denbury. Turn right here to drop down the hill towards Woodland, 1¹/₂ miles away. The telegraph poles leaning at various angles on the left-hand side of the lane look decidedly drunk. Don't try to imitate or emulate them – you will fall off your bike!

At Moorfoot Cross bear left to begin the climb past Bovey Cross and on towards Woodland. To the left, a short detour to the church of St John the Baptist is an optional extra. This building was probably constructed in 1536 when there was a great influx of quarrymen to the district, coming to work the local slates. No doubt their voluntary help was enlisted by the church.

If you decided to visit the church you will need to return to the junction and turn left. If you chose not to, carry straight on up the hill. The lane leads up and over the rise, and under pylons, before descending the steep hill to Orlycombe Bridge. Here turn left towards Landscove. The small stream to your left is part of the catchment of the River Hems, which gives its name to both Broadhempston and Littlehempston further down its valley.

Beyond Waye Farm, at the next junction, bear left. The next short section of road is not as smooth as it could be, so take care when descending the hill to the next junction. If the theory is correct that on a circular ride, done in an anticlockwise fashion, one should turn left many more times than right, then logic says we should turn left again. But, at the following junction of Wayseford Cross we show our rebellious streak by bucking that trend and turning right. About 100 yards up the slope is a rough track heading off to the left, which will take us away from surfaced roads for the best part of the next mile. The going along it will probably depend on recent weather conditions. The track skirts the lower slopes of the west face of Torcorn Hill, and runs almost parallel with the River Hems.

After a while, when you pass under a line of electricity pylons, stop and look back over your shoulder. The distant hill on the far horizon, capped by an outcrop of rocks, is Buckland Beacon on Eastern Dartmoor. In 1928 the Ten Commandments were carved on two tablets of stone here; they are still there for inspection.

Stay with the lane, ignoring a turning right by an orchard. Soon, away to the right, in the broad Hems valley ahead, you will see the immense Georgian building that is Kingston House, reputed to have the best staircase in all the kingdom!

Ten Family Bike Rides in Devon

View from Orley Common, over the countryside featured in this ride

At the end of the lane, it is no surprise to see a sign saying 'Unsuitable for Motors'. We are now at Beaston Cross, in the hamlet of Beaston. Proceed straight ahead to Broadhempston, an easy half

a mile away. The tall church tower provides the best landmark; after a short climb we semi-circumnavigate it to reach the centre of this sprawling village.

Here are the school, church, post office and a haunted pub – the Monk's Retreat. If you want to know more about this and other pubs 'licensed for spirits', then please read *Haunted Pubs in Devon*.

Follow the signs for Ipplepen, 2^1/$_2$ miles away. At Stoop Cross, turn left to pass the unusually named Coppa Dolla Inn. At Lower Well, the next junction beyond it, turn right.

The road climbs steadily to a sharp left-hand bend. Having gained the summit of the hill, there is a long downward stretch. Whilst gleefully freewheeling, you may glimpse the tower of Torbryan church, ahead to your left.

At Poole Cross, bear left to cross the Am Brook. A tributary of the River Hems, it rises in fields near Woodland, where we were earlier.

Stay with the road, which leads up the hill past Orley Common and beyond into Ipplepen. The road bends right at the church, then left down the slope of Silver Street, past the Wellington pub, bringing you back to the start.

❼ Ugborough and Modbury – A South Hams Cycle

This is a typical South Hams up-hill-and-down-dale route of about 12 miles. On this circular outing there are two short off-road sections, which will be muddy after rain. (They were when I did the ride.) The rest of the way is along high-hedged lanes, but a cyclist sees far more than a motorist.

The starting point is Ugborough, which, despite its 'unpretty' name, has won awards for 'best-kept village'. Precise details can be found on the side of the substantial bus shelter in the broad Square, where there is plenty of room to park free of charge. The detached structure is the former conduit, built in 1887, Queen Victoria's Golden Jubilee year.

About 3 miles to the east of Ivybridge, the village lies off main roads and there are many Devonians who have never been to or even heard of this lovely place.

To start the ride, heed a signpost in the centre of Ugborough that points in the general direction of Plymouth and Ermington. The road leads downhill past several attractive cottages. Ignoring a turn to the left, and another to the right, stay with it until it meets the A3121 at Haredon Cross. There is a signpost pointing to Dunwell, almost straight across this road. This is the way to go.

The next half a mile is tough because it is uphill. At first this country lane is steep but the gradient becomes gentler higher up. Dunwell is the grey building on the right with an extremely tall and steeply pitched roof. Continue past it and up to Dunwell Cross. If you have managed to ride all the way up, then you have 'done well' yourself!

Turn left at the T-junction. The prevailing wind is a south-westerly so now there may be a beneficial breeze from behind. Things become easier as the entrance to Higher Spriddlescombe Farm is passed. A short way beyond is a fork. A rough track leads off to the right here. This is the first of the two off-road sections. The first 300 yards or so are quite easy, a gentle incline on a reasonably surfaced track. However, the lane, used by farm vehicles, becomes a little softer, with the choice of a narrow left or right furrow or, perhaps, a softer, more irregular strip of green in the middle. It is at times like this that those with natural balance and genuine mountain-bike skills come into their own. I grounded my pedals on a few occasions and ended up walking.

Looking northwards over Ugborough

The views from the gateways in the vicinity of the trig point, 591 feet above sea level, are extensive. From the right gateway the sea can be glimpsed in a few places, but it is the hills that dominate the rolling South Hams landscape. From the opposite side of the lane much of southern and eastern Dartmoor, the top of Ugborough's church, Ivybridge, and parts of distant Plymouth can all be spied.

The lane is a little easier to negotiate beyond the trig point, and soon a surfaced road is met. Carry on straight ahead but only for a short distance because the B3196 cuts across our route at Longford Down Head. Stop, look and listen for traffic, particularly from the right. Take utmost care when crossing straight over onto a rough, initially level track, for the second short section of more adventurous off-road riding. This somewhat uneven, but passable, lane leads down to a surfaced road at Whetcombe Lodge. Turn left.

From here to North Huish is a pleasant downward section of about half a mile. But the easy life comes to an end deep in the valley. Needless to say, having turned to the right, it's a steep climb up the tree-lined lane to North Huish's church. But, in this apparently timeless land, there's no need to rush, so you can amble up the hill, past the monkey-puzzle tree, under a footbridge, and past an overgrown quarry to reach the hilltop church at your own pace. This is topped by an extremely pointed spire, something parachutists would be well-advised to avoid.

A junction is encountered just beyond the church. Turn right here and travel along the road for a short distance until you reach a turning on your right, by the village noticeboard. Take this right turn. A small terrace of cottages and Manor Barn are passed when travelling downhill.

Where the road bends left, head right and down the hill, where you will see a sign indicating the direction of Coombe House. The road drops down into the valley to cross a small stone bridge but beyond it rises to pass over a small knoll. Continue onwards past the drive that leads up to Coombe House.

The next half a mile is the second long climb of this ride, as the road rises up the southern side of this sheltered valley, eventually to reach a T-junction. Turn right here and ascend the hill, muscles nicely toned, lungs well filled.

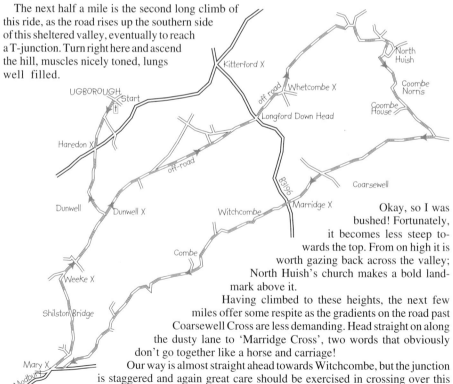

Okay, so I was bushed! Fortunately, it becomes less steep towards the top. From on high it is worth gazing back across the valley; North Huish's church makes a bold landmark above it.

Having climbed to these heights, the next few miles offer some respite as the gradients on the road past Coarsewell Cross are less demanding. Head straight on along the dusty lane to 'Marridge Cross', two words that obviously don't go together like a horse and carriage! Our way is almost straight ahead towards Witchcombe, but the junction is staggered and again great care should be exercised in crossing over this sometimes busy road, the same one as earlier.

Dropping down another long hill, you will see a distant spire directly ahead. This is the parish church of St George at Modbury. It's about 3 miles away as the crow flies.

At Witchcombe there are the remains of a manor house, where the celebrated naval commander Sir John Kempthorne was born in 1620.

Having passed Witchcombe, now a farmhouse, we find ourselves in another valley where there are many more 'combes', either in it or beside it, in the various farm names: Bearscombe, Spriddlescombe, Yarnacombe and Ley Coombe. Our last valley had been part of the drainage system of the River Avon, but the waters flowing through this deep, steep defile add their flow to the Erme.

Shilston Bridge

Although the road follows the valley it still rises, falls, twists and turns its way along. Stay with it past Spriddlescombe Manor to climb the steep hill beyond it. Well up this rise, the road that we take leads off to the right by a telegraph pole (TP 13). Soon the entrance to Croppin's Combe is reached, but decline the chance to explore the bridlepath (No 10) which passes through it. Stay with the road. Cross another stream at the bottom of the hill and then climb the other side to join the B3207 near Modbury. Turn right along it for a very short distance to reach Mary Cross.

If you want shops, toilets or pubs you may extend the ride another half a mile down into the ancient small market town of Modbury. Many liken Modbury to a small version of Totnes; there are definite topographical and architectural similarities. It is well worth a visit, but it's a stiff half a mile back up to this point to pick up the route again.

At Mary Cross turn right, almost back on yourself, to ride down the long hill to Shilston Bridge spanning the Shilston Brook. This can be crossed only if you weigh less than 17 tons!

It is now time for a further half a mile of uphill stuff. Follow the road to a T-junction, high up the hill, and turn right. Continue uphill again until Dunwell Cross is reached.

Turn left here and enjoy the easy ride back down the lane that you climbed many miles ago. At the bottom cross over the main road carefully to return to landlocked Ugborough, where there are a couple of excellent pubs whose names reflect a more maritime flavour.

Ten Family Bike Rides in Devon

❽ Broadhembury and Kentisbeare – Beneath the Blackdown Hills

This is a 14-mile country-lane ride in a semi-lowland area in the shadow of the Blackdown Hills. It may not sound madly exciting but it is a most pleasant excursion with some big views. There are no muddy tracks, just reasonably surfaced country lanes, and the only hills of any note are in the last quarter of the ride. It takes you through villages untouched by the hand of tourism. There are pubs along the way at Plymtree (Blacksmiths Arms), Kentisbeare (Wyndham Arms), and also back in Broadhembury (Drewe Arms), one of the prettiest villages in Devon.

Lying about a mile off the Honiton to Cullompton road (A373), Broadhembury is almost equidistant between these two places. Parking is not a problem as the village has a broad square. Beside it is an extremely long bench, the stretch-limo of such seats, that bears the words 'King George VI – Coronation 1937'. This is sited at the front of a small triangular grassy area.

Broadhembury

The way to cycle out of the village will probably be the same by which you drove in, along the road which runs past the Memorial Hall to the A373 at Colliton Cross. This couldn't be an easier start, as it is a case of following a gently sloping road for about three quarters of a mile. It runs parallel with the River Tale, but this watercourse isn't conspicuous from the saddle. The large house glimpsed to the right is the Grange. The Drewes lived here from 1603; its 'Oak Drawing Room' is reputed to be one of the most beautiful in Devon.

At Colliton Cross take great care when crossing straight over in the direction of Payhembury, Plymtree and Feniton; the traffic often whistles along this road even though it isn't suited to swift travel. The going beyond it is still gentle, so pedal on past Foxbeare and Heathfield to reach a junction at Egremont Cross. Turn right here towards Plymtree, two miles ahead.

Stay with this road, ignoring any turns. After a rare slope the road reaches a small stone bridge at Danes Mill to give us our first proper sight of the River Tale, a tributary of the Otter. When I passed by there was a sign asking passers-by to 'go slow' because of the presence of 'Free Range Children'.

Beyond, a slope rises all the way to Clyst William Cross. Continue straight across at this crossroads. We have now passed over a divide from the valley of the Tale, and the watershed of the Otter drainage system, to reach the upper part of the River Clyst, a tributary of the Exe. This short, almost insignificant little river has given its name to a considerable number of small settlements, cottages and farms. Examples include Clyst Hydon, Clyst St Lawrence, Broadclyst, West Clyst, Clyst St Mary, Clyst St George and Clyst William, where we are now. Clyst means 'clear stream'; said fast enough, you can see why. But don't expect to see this tiny trickle as you cycle on past the high wall of Clyst William Barton. Just beyond is an orchard, a reminder that this part of Devon was once most productive for cider apples and thereby 'Scrumpy', a heady brew responsible for the county's many 'addle-aids'! (For a definition see *An A to Z of Devonshire Dialect*.)

From a gateway on the left there is a good view across the lower lands towards Exeter. In recent decades it is this side of the county town that has seen the greatest amount of development. Fortunately, out here in the heart of the country, we are well away from this urban sprawl.

Stay with this road to pass Hayne Cross, then enjoy the gentle drop down into Plymtree. On its outskirts is the parish hall, to our left, and the village playing field to the right. Continue past the school to the Blacksmiths Arms, where, depending on the time of day, it may be possible to get some refreshment.

In the heart of the village, swing right around in front of the church of St John the Baptist, fronted by a raised pavement. A past rector, Thomas Mozley, whose incumbency spanned the years 1868–1880, was a leader-writer for *The Times*, despite 'living in the back of beyond'.

Moving on, turn left in the direction of Clyst Hydon to climb a low hill past several newish houses. Soon the next junction at Weaver Cross is reached. Turn right here, but as it is a blind bend, take extra care to listen out for approaching vehicles. You won't be able to see them – and they won't expect to see you!

Weaver Lane is named after the small River Weaver, which flows down to join the Culm near Bradninch. With grass growing in the middle in places, the lane is quiet. The going soon becomes flatter.

At Higher Weaver Cross, pass straight over the crossroads. A forking of the ways is reached in about 100 yards, at a small triangular grassy area that is Hayward's Cross. Bear left here. At the next junction, just a short distance further on, continue straight towards Clarke's Thorne, which is three quarters of a mile ahead. The lane is another pleasant one with low level fields to the side; straight ahead, and getting nearer by the minute, the high wooded western edge of the Black-down Hills can be seen.

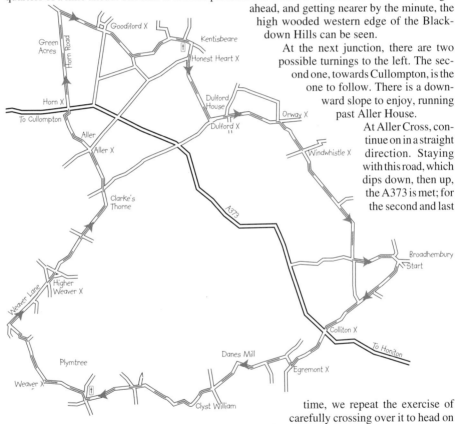

At the next junction, there are two possible turnings to the left. The second one, towards Cullompton, is the one to follow. There is a downward slope to enjoy, running past Aller House.

At Aller Cross, continue on in a straight direction. Staying with this road, which dips down, then up, the A373 is met; for the second and last time, we repeat the exercise of carefully crossing over it to head on along the straight Horn Road. We pass Horn House and Green Acres.

Near the end of the straight, cross over a small bridge spanning the River Ken. Turn right onto another straight, known as Long Drag, to cross the Ken again.

At the next crossroads (Goodiford Cross), head straight across. This is the beginning of a steepish climb, the first for ages. High up the hill, turn left to reach Kentisbeare, which takes its name from the same River Ken (plus 'beare' meaning 'wood').

Despite recent growth, the village's population almost halved between 1851 and 1961. Should you seek refreshment, the Wyndham Arms is just beyond the entrance to the church of St Mary's.

With its unusual chequered tower, the latter is also worth a visit. Until 1856, the game of Fives was regularly played against this tower. Inside the church, above the door, is a painting showing the village as seen from the hill above. There is also a framed set of pictures showing the story of the weather-vane or 'stag-bird', which was a victim of the Great Storm of 1990: it was blown from its lofty perch and badly damaged. The pictures show a happier conclusion. Look up to see it back in its rightful position atop the church. The lychgate is comparatively new, having been built in 1983 by the friends of the Honourable Vera E. Butler OBE. It commemorates her many good deeds for the church and the village.

Probably the steepest part of the ride is the section up and out of Kentisbeare; the High Street lives up to its name!

Climb past the speed restriction signs, ignoring the turn left to Blackborough at the charmingly named Honest Heart Cross. Instead, bear right towards Cullompton. At the next junction you will need to veer left towards Dulford. The going remains uphill for a while, and there are good views of the nearby hills.

The parish of Kentisbeare and Blackborough used to include 1,199 fields, but you are not expected to count them today!

The hill eventually reaches a levelling-out point. Just past Bazley's, at a gateway on the right, is a terrific view away to the south-west. From here, on a clear day, the distant hills of Dartmoor can be seen. Closer to home, the tall, majestic church tower of Cullompton stands out. To the left of that, down the Culm valley,

Kentisbeare

the distinct, wooded volcanic hill of Killerton can be spied. This is where the treasure protected by a flying dragon is buried (mentioned in an earlier ride), so if you spot it, don't be too alarmed!

Continue along this levellish road beside a tall wall concealing Dulford House. At the next road junction (Dulford Cross), turn left. At nearby Priory Wall Cross, continue straight ahead to reach the highest point on the ride. The view from here takes in about a quarter of the county.

Just as you thought you were heading up to the top of the Blackdown Hills, turn right at Orway Cross towards Broad-hembury. For the major part of the next section, the quiet lane tries to contour the hillside. We continue on as we pass the aptly named Windwhistle Cross. It is 1³/₄ miles to Broadhembury.

Ignore the left turn at Upcott Farm and continue onwards. Soon there is a long drop down to Causeway End. Turn left here and soon the tower of Broadhembury's church will be seen ahead. Cross the two-arched bridge over the River Tale to reach the centre of Broadhembury, completing a pleasant ride in a part of the county that few visitors ever see.

⑨ Chulmleigh Country – Between Exmoor and Dartmoor

It took me more than 50 years to get to Chulmleigh! It's not that the traffic was heavy or my mode of transport so slow – it's just that until now, I had no reason to go there.

It lies on a hillside above the Little Dart river, a tributary of the Taw. Despite having a population of under 2,000, I discovered it has a good range of shops, pubs (at one time it had 14!) and businesses. This is probably because it has no major towns (or out-of-town supermarkets) as competition on its doorstep: it is left to fend for itself.

The village is roughly midway between Crediton and Barnstaple. Having found your way there, park in the free car park in New Street; this is by a tall wall bounding the precincts of the parish church.

From the car park head right and up New Street to the crossroads in the centre of the 'town'.

Continue straight over and along East Street. This will take you onwards and out of Chulmleigh past the oldest Congregational Chapel in Devon.

Soon you will begin a steep descent to the diminutive Huntacott Bridge. The only serious upwards hill of the entire 13-mile ride is now confronted. Ignore a minor road off to the right, and stick with what appears to be the main drag.

The conquering of this hill has its reward. A tableland with many miles of fairly level, pleasant, easy riding lies ahead. On reaching Huntacott Farm, it is important that you heed the signs and don't run down the ducks. Equally important, don't fall in either or both of the duck ponds!

For the next five miles stay with this road. Do not turn off at Edgiford Cross, Stone Moor Cross, Cheldon Cross, Benley Cross, Bealey Court Cross, Molland Cross or even Mouseberry Cross. Enjoy the surroundings and the occasional views. You will also have to watch out for game birds: I encountered at least twenty in this section.

You will know when it is time to leave this road, as at Burrow Cross you will encounter the first set of 'give way' signs to go against you.

Turn left here towards Meshaw and Alswear.

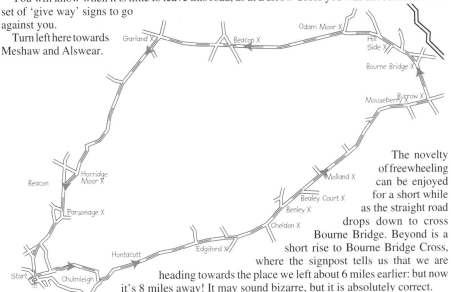

The novelty of freewheeling can be enjoyed for a short while as the straight road drops down to cross Bourne Bridge. Beyond is a short rise to Bourne Bridge Cross, where the signpost tells us that we are heading towards the place we left about 6 miles earlier: but now it's 8 miles away! It may sound bizarre, but it is absolutely correct.

Bear left, this being achieved by staying with the same road and not taking the one right to Meshaw. Do the same and also bear left at Meshaw Moor Cross. You will now pass a number of properties on your right, the sign telling you to be aware of the possibility of people walking on the highway. Beyond, at Hillside Cross, ignore the road to the right and bear left again.

Having travelled east in the first part of the ride, we now head westwards, the road more undulating than earlier but with no gradients of any severe steepness. Continue on the same road past Odam Moor Cross.

In about another mile, you will know that you are reaching Beacon Cross as beacons are invariably on the highest ground. The gateway to the right near the summit provides northward views to Exmoor, whilst the one just beyond on the left has southward views to the more distant hills and tors of Dartmoor. To the left of this it is possible to pick out the hills that are on the edge of Exeter. It is a terrific view.

Stay with the road; do not take either of the two roads to the left by Beacon Cross. Continue down the slope, across the col, and up the other side to Garland Cross. Ignore the two dogs on sentry duty at the Wishing Well: they won't bite. The views from here are also magnificent. Turn left. The signpost points to the two 'leighs': Chaw and Chulm. 'Leigh' in a place-name usually means 'in a wood', but the trees are not in evidence today.

Beacon

Beyond a short rise there is a lovely downhill section over Long Moor. To a degree this easy going is evened out by a rise, in a few miles, up to Horridge Moor Cross, then onwards on the same road to Chulmleigh Beacon.

Here there is a modern beacon, albeit on a pole. A quite magnificent view is to be enjoyed away to the west where the land just falls away to a patchwork-quilt of beautiful countryside.

Bear left. The signpost points the way to Chulmleigh; it's downhill all the way! Ignoring two roads to the left, veer left at the college, then at the crossroads in the centre of Chulmleigh, turn right into New Street to relocate your vehicle.

Chulmleigh, a former wool town, dates back to Saxon times; if you have the energy, why not have a look round? You may be pleasantly surprised at what it has to offer.

⑩ Exeter – River Exe and Exeter Canal (the flat bits!)

At about 12 miles long, this is a relatively short, easy, flat ride: the perfect way to end this interactive book. The starting point is yet another free car park: a rarity in Exeter. If you are unfamiliar with the layout of the city, it may take cute cartographical skills in order to locate the starting point. It is in Station Road, in the Exwick district of Exeter. If you get to St David's railway station, you are almost there. From the Great Western Hotel, near the station, turn left to follow Cowley Bridge Road. In the shortest of distances you will see a level crossing on the left, which you must cross. Beyond is Station Road; it first passes over the River Exe and then, just a short distance further on, crosses a flood relief channel. Beside this, on the left side of the road, is a small car park. If it is full, try to park further along the road on the right-hand side.

Here we are at the northern end of a cycle route that more or less follows the River Exe and the Exeter Canal. Travel to the right, southwards, from this car park along the edge of the flood relief channel. This low-lying part of the city was once prone to flooding; the worst of these inundations occurred in late October 1960. The perennial floods had to be tamed, so in the 1970s this curving deep depression was constructed to accommodate flood waters.

The 'Exe Cycle Way' heads away from the water-filled dyke, then soon veers left towards 'Exe Bridges and City Centre'. The sports ground to your right belongs to the Civil Service; beyond it are allotments that we skirt before dipping down to pass under the main railway line.

The cycle path now curves around to the concrete banks of the River Exe, arriving close to both a pair of weirs and pedestrian bridges. The more ornate of the two is 'Millers' Crossing'. Do not cross them. Continue along the man-made river bank in the demarcated cycle lane. This aerial picture shows the area ahead of us on the next part of this ride.

The two traffic-choked Exe Bridges, North and South, are soon reached but they do not cause us any bother. We simply pass beneath them on our carefree, traffic-free way along the river bank. Beyond the second bridge there is a steep ramp to pass up and over, but with the right momentum it's not much of an obstacle. The small terrace of six houses beside it is called Gervase Avenue; it is named after the medieval benefactor who funded the first stone bridge across the River Exe. What's left of his many-arched bridge is found on the other side of the river. Its size suggests that when it was built, the river was three times wider, but only a third as deep.

Continue on and behind the back of the Malthouse family pub to cycle past a children's playground. Keeping the Exe to the left, hog the river bank as it gracefully curves round to reach the suspended, pedestrian Cricklepit Bridge. Again, don't cross it. It is named after a small street that ran beneath the base of the city wall and loosely means 'the street beneath the cliff'.

If this is your first visit to Exeter Quay, and you have a feeling of déjà-vu, then it may be explained by the fact that Exeter shared with Dartmouth the role of Victorian Liverpool in the BBC's *The Onedin Line,* and the tall warehouses opposite featured in many shots. The filmmakers also liked to confuse the locals, for there were scenes which defied belief. For example, Mrs Onedin stood on Exeter Quay waving a fond farewell to her husband as he sailed out of the mouth of the Dart, some 40 miles away!

The maritime theme continues, as for three decades the Maritime Museum occupied various premises centred on the Canal Basin (completed in 1830), soon seen on the right. Sadly it closed in 1997; at the time of writing (2004), the future and face of this part of the city was being rigorously debated.

Continue along the river until an entrance, opposite the Port Royal pub, to the Exeter Canal is reached. Now it is a case of crossing the left one of two bridges over the sluice gates. Head up the

River Exe

left bank of the canal, under the shadow of the tastefully painted (to blend in with the scenery?) gasometers or gas holders. Just about 100 yards beyond them, bear left to follow the cycle way, which proceeds at a midpoint between river and canal. Don't turn left towards the 'Match Factory' suspension bridge.

This is the Riverside Valley Park, a pleasant green corridor and a favoured playground of walkers, dog walkers, canoeists and cyclists. Your patience may be tried – pedestrians, despite the dedicated walkways and cycle lanes, often seem oblivious as to who should be where. Try not to run down anyone who has erred from the footpath…

Having passed soccer pitches, the cycle way swings right after several hundred yards to reach the canal, where a small bridge leads to Clapperbrook Lane. Don't cross it. Turn left to follow the canal to the Double Locks pub, about half a mile away. There is a 10 mph speed limit.

This character pub has a super beer garden, with a volleyball court, and is extremely popular with young people. On a warm summer's evening, it can get very busy.

The onward ride to the southern end of the Canal at the Turf Hotel is straightforward. The purpose-built cycle path runs to the left of the Double Locks; in another half a mile it reaches the Countess Wear swing bridge on the Exeter By-Pass.

Here, turn right and ride along the pavement over the swing bridge to reach the far bank. Pedestrian-controlled traffic lights enable the Exeter By-Pass to be safely crossed. The towpath southwards is initially very narrow, so pedestrians must take precedence. But don't worry, the path gets wider to become a most pleasant waterside route under the M5 bridge and down to the Turf Hotel at the canal's southern end. Along the way, good views are obtained over waterfront Topsham, on the eastern side of the estuary, whilst to the right the low-lying Exminster Marshes form one of the largest areas of flat land in Devon.

The Turf Hotel is seasonal and makes an unusual place to take a break. From the small park-like peninsula of the hotel grounds, there are wonderful views down the widening Exe estuary towards Exmouth and Dawlish Warren.

At the Double Locks

The return journey from the Turf Hotel back to the start is the same route in reverse; it should be a formality. The reverse views will be different, Exeter Cathedral becoming far more noticeable as a landmark. For the shortest of detours, Exeter Quay is worthy of an extended visit. There is an interpretation centre complete with free slide presentation of the city's history.

Double Locks

Opposite this there's an antique and collectables centre situated in the former fish market. Also, there are several clubs, pubs and eating places.

I hope you will safely enjoy these 'family bike rides' and that they will show you some of the county's lesser-visited countryside: the real Devon!

I also trust that you have not been too troubled by that far-from-extinct prehistoric cycling monster known as the 'extremely-saurus'!

Exeter Canal

Turf Hotel, Exeter Canal